The Silver Lining

The Silver Lining

NANCY WILSON

canonpress
Moscow, Idaho

Published by Canon Press
P.O. Box 8729, Moscow, ID 83843
800.488.2034 | www.canonpress.com

Cover design by James Engerbretson
Interior design by Valerie Anne Bost
Printed in the United States of America.

Unless otherwise indicated, Scripture quotations are from the King James Version of the Bible.

Library of Congress Cataloging-in-Publication Data
Wilson, Nancy, 1952- author.
The silver lining : a practical guide for Christian grandmothers / Nancy Wilson.
Moscow : Canon Press, 2018. | Includes bibliographical references and index.
LCCN 2018024527 | ISBN 194450379X (pbk. : alk. paper)
LCSH: Grandmothers—Religious life.
Classification: LCC BV4847 .W55 2018 | DDC 248.8/431—dc23
LC record available at https://lccn.loc.gov/2018024527

16 17 18 19 20 21 22   10 9 8 7 6 5 4 3 2

To Anita, Diane, and Judy,
godly mothers who share dear descendants with me.

CONTENTS

Look for the Silver Lining

Whatever season of life we are in, God's promises continue to be new every morning. As we transition into being the "older women" in the church, we want to be the kind of older women who are characterized by godly wisdom and great joy in the life God has given us.

When I was a young woman, I looked forward to having gray hair because, I thought, surely by then I would have wisdom! But obviously, I knew more was required than simple age. I would need to walk faithfully day by day to acquire a good and godly wisdom. And as the gray hairs started appearing, I decided they were not gray after all, but silver.

Proverbs 16:31 says, "The silver-haired is a crown of glory, if it is found in the way of righteousness." There it is: the big IF. If we have silver hair, it is only a crown of glory if it is traveling "in the way" on the road of holiness. And even if this part of the road has some rough spots, there is a silver lining around every hardship, and that silver lining is the joy of the Lord.

So this book is for those women who are traveling, as I am, through the seasons of life with the desire to grow in grace and wisdom, with the goal to keep pressing on to be fruitful and faithful. And having passed the height of summer, and now somewhere in the autumn season, we want to look forward to all that is coming with courage. We want to continue to do our duties faithfully and cheerfully, not shrinking back, but embracing each day with thanks and humility, keeping on "the way of righteousness."

Psalm 90:12 says, "So teach us to number our days, that we may apply our hearts unto wisdom." Notice that the purpose of numbering our days is so we can apply wisdom. We tend to number our days by counting down how many shopping days are left until Christmas, or how long until our daughter's due date, or a coming wedding or other important event. But none of us knows how many days are left on the calendar of our earthly life. Even so, we are

to number them. How do we do this? The psalm-
ist asks God to teach us. And when He does, we
can apply our hearts to wisdom.This means study-
ing wisdom, looking for wisdom the way Proverbs
2:4–5 describes for us: "If you seek her as silver,
and search for her as for hidden treasures; then you
will understand the fear of the Lord, and find the
knowledge of God."

FAITH

Faith is still the central thing we need, whether for
this part of the journey or for what lies ahead. Paul's
concluding exhortation in 1 Corinthians sums it up
nicely: "Watch, stand fast in the faith, be brave, be
strong" (1 Cor. 16:13).

My mother-in-law used to compare faith to a mus-
cle: the more we use faith, the stronger it gets. And
it's important to keep limber and flexible, right? Exercising our faith means trusting God, obeying Him,
expecting Him to do as He promised. So, walking by
faith is the way we walk through the entire Christian life. It is not a special secret that He will reveal
to us if we are good. It is basic Christian living.

In Ephesians 2:10 Paul says, "For we are his work-
manship, created in Christ Jesus unto good works,
which God hath before ordained that we should
walk in them."

In all seasons of life, God has good works pre-pared in advance for us to walk in. Whether you are a young woman, married, unmarried, widowed, middle-aged, newly married, or a great-grandma, you never quit exercising faith in Christ, you never quit doing the good works He has designed for you. This is the Christian life: keeping our eyes on Christ, not on ourselves, not on the circumstances, but do-ing our duties at each stage, from our birth until our death. This is the walk of faith.

STAND FAST

"Be strong and of good courage, fear not, nor be afraid of them: for the Lord thy God, he it is that doth go with thee; he will not fail thee, nor forsake thee" (Deut. 31:6).

Older women sometimes give way to worry, fear, and anxious thoughts. But I think the reason we do this is because that is what we have done all along. If we worried as young women, then we will continue to worry. But in older women, it ought not to be. We have had long years of experience of the Lord's good-ness, so we of all women should be courageous and stand fast in the faith. What does it mean to stand fast? It means we don't budge.

"Finally, my brethren, be strong in the Lord, and in the power of His might" (Eph. 6:10). This strength we need is found in the Lord, not in ourselves. It is His might, and certainly not ours. Otherwise, we would have good reason to be fearful!   ⸴

AND JOY OVER ALL!

As we look for the silver lining as we grow older, let's keep Psalm 5:11–12 as an inspiration before us:

"But let all those rejoice who put their trust in You; let them ever shout for joy, because You defend them; let those also who love Your name be joyful in You. For You, O Lord, will bless the righteous; with favor You will surround him as with a shield."

Understanding
Who We Are in Christ

Whenever we turn to discuss our individual callings and duties (whether as mothers, daughters, or grandmas), it's important to first review, understand, and settle in our minds the foundational truths of who we are in Christ. It's possible to get distracted away from some very basic principles when we find ourselves in new territory. But no matter what our age or circumstances, biblical principles remain the same. Thankfully, God has not laid out a new set of standards for our older years. He is the same yesterday, today, and forever (Heb. 13:8).

The Christian life is the same from start to finish. It is a walk of faith, no matter what part of the road we are traveling. We continue to put one foot in front of the other, just as we always have, trusting God as we go. Sure, we are in new territory. But all of life has been new territory! Old age is actually a sign of God's blessing. Remember the first command with a promise? "Honor your father and mother which is the first commandment with promise: that it may be well with you and you may live long on the earth" (Eph. 6:2–3).

WHO ARE WE?

Thankfully, in a world mixed up, it is our Creator who defines us. Who else could possibly know who we are and what we were made for but our Creator? We don't define ourselves, and neither does the world, despite its ongoing attempts to do so. We must listen to the Word. The Bible tells us we are created in the image of God, redeemed by the blood of Jesus Christ, forgiven of our sins, reconciled to God, and sealed with the Holy Spirit of promise.

"In Him you also trusted, after you heard the word of truth, the gospel of your salvation; in whom also, having believed, you were sealed with the Holy Spirit of promise,who is the guarantee of our inheritance until the redemption of the purchased possession, to the praise of His glory" (Eph. 1:13–14).

This is the starting point for everything else that follows: we heard, we trusted, we believed, we were sealed. This is great news!

Galatians 2:20: "I have been crucified with Christ; it is no longer I who live, but Christ lives in me; and the life which I now live in the flesh I live by faith in the Son of God, who loved me and gave Himself for me." What a joy to know it is "no longer I who live, but Christ lives in me"? We are united with Christ. He lives in us, and this is a living union, characterized by close fellowship with Him. It is a dynamic relationship, not a static state. We are to be growing in Him.

"He has delivered us from the power of darkness and conveyed us into the kingdom of the Son of His love, in whom we have redemption through His blood, the forgiveness of sins" (Col. 1:13–14).

We are subjects in the Kingdom of the Son. We no longer serve under the banner of darkness and sin, but under the banner of redemption and love.

We don't need to "reinvent ourselves." We don't need to have an identity crisis. We know who we are in Christ, we know who our Father is, where we came from, what we are for, where we are now, and where we are going. That is actually huge! I remember back in the 1970s young people were trying to "find themselves." Apart from Christ, we really are lost. In Christ, we are truly "found."

This quote from Kenneth Boa's *Handbook to Prayer* puts it in a nutshell:

> To love ourselves correctly is to see ourselves as God sees us and to allow the Word, not the world, to define us by telling us who and whose we really are. The clearer we capture the vision of our new identity in Christ, the more we will realize that our deepest needs for security, significance, and satisfaction are met in Him and not in people, possessions, or positions.*

So let's push this into the corners.

OUR IDENTITY IS IN CHRIST.

We are defined by Him, not by our culture, not by what we do.

Women tend to define themselves by what they do. And this motivates women to adopt externals to "belong." I suppose we could call it a tribal impulse. We want to belong to a group and let that define us. We might look to be part of a group based on our job: I'm a mom, a wife, a nurse, a teacher, a designer, a bookkeeper, a baker, a grandma. Or we could look for the same thing by our hobbies: working out at the gym, joining a quilting group, running marathons, or opening a soup kitchen. Now these are all great things in

---

* Kenneth Boa, *Handbook to Prayer* (Atlanta: Trinity House, 1993).

themselves, but they are all secondary. None of these jobs or hobbies or endeavors can bear the weight of providing meaning and purpose for our lives. They are all finite, as we are. Some day we might not be able to do these things anymore. Then what?

If we let ourselves be defined merely by what we do, then we are at sea when we are not doing those things anymore. When the kids grow up, we have the empty-nest syndrome. When we retire from our job, we get restless after a few months. When our husband dies, we don't know who we are anymore. But we are in Christ! That has not changed.

OUR NEED TO FEEL NEEDED

We all have a basic need to feel needed by someone, and certainly this is a God-given need. It is not evil. But we can look for our personal value or significance in the wrong places. In other words, if we feel needed at work or if we know our kids need us, we can begin to look to them to make us feel important. But we can be fired or replaced at work. Our kids grow up and don't need us to hover over them or care for them the same way. This can lead to disappointment. We can be overlooked, under-thanked, misunderstood, unappreciated. Someone (important) forgot our birthday. No one noticed how hard we worked to prepare a meal. No one compliments us anymore. We may feel minimized, unimportant, not needed. And of course these feelings can lead to self-pity, attributing motives, and more disappointment.

But if we find all our significance in Christ, those things we do are offered up to Him as a means of thanking Him for His goodness and kindness to us. He has made us for a purpose. He has created good works for us to do, and He has created enough to last our entire lifetime. This elevates the significance and importance of all we do. Rather than finding value in being successful at our work or in our homes, we find our value in pleasing God. He made us for a purpose, and He enables us to fulfill it. So our callings as grandmas or wives or mothers become more significant, not less, when we recognize them as not the source of our fulfillment. Unmarried women need to understand this too. They will not find their ultimate needs met in marriage or childbearing, and knowing this frees them to enjoy who they are in Christ as whole women.

OUR NEED TO FEEL SECURE

Security is not found in a blanket we carry around, but we might be actually viewing our husband, children, job, house, health, bank account, friendships, or dress size like a security blanket. These are very unreliable sources of security. Husbands die, children grow up, jobs end, houses get old, bank accounts fluctuate, friendships can drift, health can change, and dress sizes are very fickle things. We feel anxious and worried about many things if we put our trust in earthly creatures or things. The older we get, the more there is to worry about. So it is better to decide right now to forsake worry. It is like taking ugly pills anyway. Worry robs us of our sense of peace and skews our perspective.

The future can cause insecurity because we don't know what's coming. If we try to anticipate every contingency and have a plan for every possibility, we can run ourselves ragged. Remember, all worry begins with two words: What if? Don't do traffic in "what if" questions. Ignore suggestions of that nature because you can't answer them anyway! What if I get cancer? What if I don't?

In Christ we are safe. He defends and protects us. He will never leave us or forsake us. We have rock-solid promises, certainty, and assurance in Him. We can cast all our cares on Him for He cares for us. He knows the future and He will be there for and with us.

OUR NEED TO FEEL SATISFIED

True fulfillment is not going to be found in worldly success, as attractive as it seems. And by success I mean yours or your husband's or your children's, whether it be in wealth, education, athletics, promotions, reputation, relationships, success, beauty, health, or popularity. These are all earthly and very temporary, and they can change or disappear in a flash. Don't let your hearts and minds be focused on things on the earth, but on things above, where Christ is. When we are giving our attention to these worldly things, then we are not giving Christ our all. If we focus on these fleeting things, we are set up to worry over them. If we strive for all this earthly stuff, it will drive out our desire for God.

Looking for fulfillment in people or stuff brings restlessness, dissatisfaction, and makes us discontent. You might know people like this, who are always adrift, always looking for something, never sure of their direction or purpose, moving here, moving there, and never finding paradise.

But Christ is the only source of true fulfillment. We can't look to our husbands to fulfill all our wants and needs and desires. Think of the tremendous burden that puts on them! We must look to Christ. We don't look to our retirement package or health insurance to give us security. They won't!

None of our deepest needs for these things (significance, security, and fulfillment) can be met in people (what a burden to put on them) or in our stuff (what a foolish idea) or in our positions (which are changeable).*

The Word defines our ultimate purpose, not the world. The world is always telling us what we should look like, how we should spend our money and our time, how we should dress, and what we should eat (and not eat). The target is always moving, and we can never finally arrive to the place of satisfaction. The world wants the glory that belongs only to God. In fact, worldliness is giving the world the glory that belongs to God.

When we let God's Word define us, we can find fulfillment derivatively from the things (good works) He has given us to do because we are fulfilled in Christ first. Living this way sets us free to enjoy the life He has given us in each and every stage. Knowing who we are gives us confidence and joy and courage.

---

* Boa, *A Handbook to Prayer*.

CHAPTER 2

The Older Women

Quite a lot has been written about the passage in Titus 2 describing the duties of older (aged) women in the church. Though the charge to the older women seems clear enough, the implementation can be challenging. I'd like to consider this passage in light of the culture and times we live in and address some things for us "aged" women to consider.

Here is the relevant passage in Titus 2:3–5: "The older women likewise, that they be reverent in behavior, not slanderers, not given to much wine, teachers of good things - that they admonish the young women to love their husbands, to love their children, to be discreet, chaste, homemakers, good, obedient to their own husbands, that the word of God may not be blasphemed."

First of all, who are the older women? These are the women who have grown children, women who have successfully raised a family and now have the time (and probably the resources) to bestow on others outside their own families.

In our American culture, once the children are raised and out the door, women can feel displaced and unsure of their calling. This is particularly true among the women who have been home-centered all those years when the home was full of little children. But even if a woman maintains close contact with her children after they leave home, her responsibilities have shifted, to say the least. Many women in this age group take on jobs either for financial reasons or simply to be productive and useful. Those who don't want to be tied down by a job can fritter away their time and money if they don't find a useful occupation of their gifts and resources. And those with paying jobs can be too busy to be helping the younger women in the church.

Once I spoke with a young woman who was frustrated because she felt none of the older women in her church were available to the younger women because they were all either working full time or were consumed with themselves. She said that most of the older women in her church had personal trainers, were constantly at the gym or shopping or traveling or spending time at the spa, getting tan and manicured. They simply were not available. I have thought that her perspective might have been exaggerated, but I know the problem really does exist in some (affluent) places.

Worldliness has a constant tug on us. We need to be aware and wary. When women look to the world instead of to the Bible for direction, it's no wonder they become distracted. And it is fun to be cut loose from the heavy responsibilities of mothering after twenty-some odd years. So it is a very predictable temptation for women to head off to do some of the things they were unable to do back when the kids were little. And of course, some of this is fine. Having free time can be a reward for a job well done, as long as it isn't taken too far. At the same time, if the older women collect in exclusive groups and shut themselves off from the younger women, this most certainly will not contribute to the general welfare of the church community. Older women have much to offer, whether they realize it or not!

Sometimes the opposite is the case: the older women feel cut out of the loop with the younger women. The young women are in the middle of having babies, and that's pretty much all they want to talk about: pregnancy, nursing, childbirth, etc. The older women can grow weary of it. After all, they've already done all that, and they are ready to move on to something else. But, to be fair, the older women can do the same thing. They can talk of their ailments or how to care for their elderly parents, and the young women can feel bored to tears. In other words, this is really about living sacrificially. The young women need to try to connect with the older women, and vice versa.

Often the older women would love to be a help or encouragement to the younger women, but they have no idea how to begin. Or they feel they don't really have anything to offer. But they do! They don't have any real contact with the younger women, and the younger women are not asking them for advice but are seeking out women in their own age group. So let's go back to the text in Titus and see if we can sort some of this out.

First we need to consider the qualifications for the older women that Titus lists. Paul doesn't say that all aged women should be teaching the younger women. Age is not the only qualification. They are to be "reverent in behavior, not slanderers, not given to much wine, teachers of good things." In other words, they have to have something to say based on a lifetime of holiness.

Reverent in Behavior

The King James says "likewise, that they be in behavior as becometh holiness." That really sums it up. We are to be the kind of women whose lives are characterized by holiness.

The word likewise means that this behavior encompasses all that has been mentioned in the previous verses to the men: "That the older men be sober, reverent, temperate, sound in faith, in love, in patience." We do not have a separate list of virtues for women. We are to live, speak, dress, and behave Christianly, just like the men must. That is to be the standard for our conduct. Let's do a quick review of these virtues mentioned for the old men before we turn back to the older women.

Sober: In old age, given the presence of aches and pains, there might be a temptation to over-indulge. But we must stay on track, remembering that we are setting an example to the younger saints. We are not given a free pass to get a little tipsy.

Reverent: An older woman who is acting or dressing or driving or dancing like a twenty-year-old is a sad sight. My son-in-law calls them day-old donuts. When I was in college, "Moms' Weekend" brought lots of mothers into town. I was so grateful that my mother was such a gracious woman, especially in contrast to some who were dressed like silly teenagers. She was respectable, courteous, and reverent.

Temperate: We older women should not lurch from one extreme to another, but be predictable, steady, emotionally self-governed, and not easily lead astray.

Sound in faith: We ought to be theologically educated. We need to be Bible readers and Bible students. This keeps us growing and equips us to be fruitful.

And now to those characteristics assigned specifically to the older women.

Not slanderers: This is a command to watch what we say. We are to guard our tongues, not believe everything we hear or read on social media, and not pass on hearsay willy-nilly. Think of how much the internet word count would drop if this were put into practice!

Not given to much wine: This is pretty straight forward. Older women are singled out to watch it with the wine intake. This does not mean no wine; that would be easy. But this means we must use wisdom to govern how much. Too much wine opens us up to other sins. This saying sums it up nicely: "The man takes a drink; the drink takes a drink; the drink takes the man." Be moderate. Be self-controlled.

TEACHERS OF GOOD THINGS

Paul warns Timothy (1 Timothy 1:6–7) of those who "having swerved have turned aside unto vain jangling. Desiring to be teachers of the law; understanding neither what they say, nor whereof they affirm" (KJV). I confess that I love that phrase: vain jangling. It is so descriptive! Women who are not qualified to teach, who have "swerved" away from the faith, are vain janglers. You can see it all over the internet without even trying. Let's be guarded, careful, thoughtful, and measure our words so they are rich with God's truth and not like a lot of clanging and jangling. Then we will be equipped to offer encouragement to the young women who are so hungry for it.

Often older women go straight to verse 4 of Titus 2 and wonder why the young women are not flocking around to be taught. But we must carefully consider the qualifications we are to have first.

Since we will soon turn to the duties of the grandma, we must get this basic law in our minds: if you are a good, gracious Christian woman, you will obviously be a good and gracious mother-in-law and grandma. If you are a fuss-budget Christian, you will be a fuss-budget grandma. If you are intemperate in your habits as a Christian woman, you will be an intemperate grandma. Obviously, we want to live "as becometh holiness" like Sarah. Then we will be the kind of grandmas who are assets to our families and bring God glory.

CHAPTER 3

A Marriage Refresher

For wives, our duties to our husbands remain fairly straightforward after the children grow up and move on to establish families of their own. Even so, those basic wifely duties adjust and adapt to our age, our husband's calling, and our circumstances. Even (or especially) after forty years or so, it always good to go back to the basics for a refresher. We can easily start to coast, and we need reminders to keep at our posts and not slack off. We should adopt the attitude of an expert, who sees that she is finally getting good at this job.

The Virtuous Wife

Let's look at that proverbial wife of Proverbs 31. Rather than looking at the whole chapter here, I want to concentrate on just two verses (10–12): "Who can find a virtuous wife? For her worth is far above rubies. The heart of her husband safely trusts her; she will have no lack of gain. She does him good and not evil all the days of her life."

From these two verses alone we see that she has two important (and impressive) characteristics: Her husband trusts her, and she is a constant source of good to him.

Our first duty is to be trustworthy. We ought to be the kind of women our husbands trust implicitly. We are trustworthy with the home, with the finances, with all we promise to do, and we discharge those duties faithfully. How do we do this? Because we trust God. If we did not trust God, we would not be trustworthy ourselves.

Our husbands should not have to be "checking on us" to see if we spent our day productively. They should be so confident in us (safely trusting us) that they don't need to ask themselves or us such questions. They know that we strive to be obedient to God, that we are women of the Word, faithful and fruitful. This comes of years, even decades, of a good testimony. When we have broken our husband's trust in a serious way, it might take a while to earn it back again. But if we confess our sins to God, He forgives us, and by God's grace, our husbands can forgive us as well. But our goal should be to live in such a manner that we don't give our husbands any occasion to worry.

The second thing we see in these verses is that we are commissioned to bring our husbands good and not evil. When do we do this? How often? All the days of our lives. Not just as newlyweds or in our twenties or thirties, but "all the days" of our lives. This is an everyday obligation. Do you have time on your hands? Then reflect on this: How are you bringing your husband good today? We bring our husbands good with our attitude and demeanor, our labor and diligence, and our affection and love. There is no end of good we can bring to our husbands. A ruby is a beautiful gem, but a wife like this is beyond the value of rubies. The thing that makes a stone precious is its beauty and rarity. Likewise, a trustworthy wife who brings her husband good is beautiful, valuable, and rare.

The S Word

Colossians 3:18: "Wives, submit to your own husbands as is fitting in the Lord."

Ephesians 5:22–24: "Wives, submit to your own husbands, as to the Lord. For the husband is head of the wife, as also Christ is head of the church; and He is the Savior of the body. Therefore, just as the church is subject to Christ, so let the wives be to their own husbands in everything."

1 Peter 3:1: "Wives, likewise, be submissive to your own husbands..."

There are several important things about this command for wives to be submissive. First, the command is to the wives, not their husbands. It does not say, "Husbands, see that your wives are submissive." This is important. Second, wives are to be submissive to their own husbands. The command is exclusive; it is for each wife to submit to her own husband, not to someone else's husband. And third, this submission is to be rendered "as to the Lord." This means that our submission to our own husband is modeled after our submission to the Lord. That, my friends, is a very tall order and no joke. But if you feel like it's impossible, take a look at the command to the husbands in Ephesians: they are told to love their wives as Christ loved the church and gave Himself for her. They model their own behavior after Christ as well.

So both wives and husbands have impossible jobs. But remember that we find in Christ all the resources we need to obey all He commands. We certainly don't find the resources in ourselves or in our own strength.

Submission is a bad word in our culture today because it has many ungodly associations. But biblical submission is in a different category that the world cannot understand. Submission is a holy thing because we see Christ submitting to the will of His Father. He has given us a model by showing us how to do this. His submission was exclusively to His Father. He willingly submitted, laying His life down. So let's give ourselves a good job description here. When we willingly submit to our own husbands, we are following our good Savior in this duty. Let's define our submission to our own husbands as a cheerful acceptance of his leadership and headship.

Often we do cheerfully accept his leadership, but we may be tempted to argue or try to steer and direct with our "helpful suggestions" to go another route. This amounts to a rejection of his leadership. And certainly, a grumpy acceptance of his leadership is not a biblical submission. Be a cheerful follower, a sheep who is happy to follow the shepherd. Let's make it a joy for our husbands to lead us.

Though the angel Gabriel appeared to Mary to tell her the astonishing news that she would bear the Messiah, all future appearances (via dreams) was to Joseph. God sent His directions to Joseph to pack up and get the mother and the baby out of town (in the middle of the night) and off to Egypt. And then

Joseph was told when to return and where. So I expect that God is going to lead me through my husband as well. He will get the word when it is time to move on.

This does not mean that I view my husband as a mediator between me and God. I have my own relationship with God through Christ. I pray, I confess, I worship, and I read. But as far as my marriage goes, I expect God will move our household through my husband's leadership. We may discuss things at length, but finally, I trust that God will wake Doug up in the night if we are supposed to head off to Egypt. I just hope I will be as cooperative as Mary apparently was!

So let's talk a bit about application now. Here's a question for you. How are you doing with following your husband? Do you take his advice seriously? Has he suggested or requested that you to do something that you haven't done yet? Do you drag your feet or complain about his decisions? Or do you joyfully, cheerfully follow him the same way you follow Christ?

Sometimes as we get older, we can think we don't have to be submissive anymore. That's for the new wives, we think, not for the older, wiser ones. But this is false (and funny). Surely we are not falling for that one! We are to bring our husbands good all the days of our life. God's command to us is not based on our age or experience. We are to walk in cheerful, joyful obedience always.

RESPECT

Ephesians 5:33: "Nevertheless, let each one of you in particular so love his own wife as himself, and let the wife see that she respects her husband." This command is also directed to the wife. We are to oversee ourselves in this department of respecting our husbands. Let's quickly review what respect means. How do we do this? Is it just a feeling? No. It is a manner of our conversation and behavior, not a feeling. The words that come to mind that should characterize our conversation and behavior toward our husbands are honor, courtesy, kindness, and deference. We are to remember the role he has been assigned as our head and treat him accordingly. All the way to the end. This can be very challenging if your husband is not respectable. But even in the worst cases, even if you must separate from him, you can still treat him with courtesy and kindness. And remember that all our respect and submission is ultimately rendered to God, and we know that He always blesses obedience.

Once an older woman told me that she couldn't show respect to her husband now because he

wouldn't know what to do if she did. He might laugh
at her. He might wonder what got into her. But it is
never too late to do what God has told us to do. It
may take courage and humility to begin, but better
late than never.

CONJUGAL LOVE

Song of Solomon 8:6–7: "Set me as a seal upon your
heart, as a seal upon your arm...many waters cannot
quench love, nor can the floods drown it. If a man
would give for love all the wealth of his house, it
would be utterly despised."

If floods can't drown love, then certainly old age
cannot drown it either!

Genesis 18:12: "Therefore Sarah laughed within
herself, saying, 'After I have grown old, shall I have
pleasure, my lord being old also?'"

Sarah had grown old. She was worn out. And
Abraham was old too. But Sarah still described con-
jugal love as having pleasure. We should enjoy the
pleasures of the marriage bed as long as we can.
Though we might grow too old and infirm to enjoy it like we did in our younger years, that should
not necessarily be a problem to fix. We are not to be
idolatrous about the marriage bed. At some point,
you are going to wear out and your husband is going to wear out, too. The world may try to sell us all

kinds of extensions on the warranty, but the truth is, we are finite creatures. The marriage bed should always be a place of communion, comfort, and joy. It should always be a pleasure. But don't put pressure on your husband, and don't ignore your husband. Be a joyful wife even after you have grown old. As desires wane, ask God to rekindle them. Give to one another in the Lord. God is good.

LITTLE FOXES

Song of Songs 2:15: "Catch us the foxes, the little foxes that spoil the vines, for our vines have tender grapes."

It is often the case that the little foxes spoil the garden of our marriage more than the backhoes. We allow little hindrances to creep in, and they can actually do quite a bit of damage. Here are three examples of little foxes we should look out for.

WORLDLY NOTIONS

The marriage bed is honorable, and we are to hold it in honor. One way to honor it is to keep the world's false notions about sex and what is sexy out of the marriage bed. We are aging, and we can't compete with immodest twenty-year-olds. We should not even try. We are to grow in wisdom about ourselves and our husbands and our relationship with him. Don't compare yourself to yourself at twenty. Don't compare yourself to the world's "ideal" woman. In fact, don't compare yourself, period. Get over yourself and invite your husband to enjoy you as you enjoy him.

BAD HABITS

You may have old patterns of misbehavior, bad habits that need to be broken. They may be little foxes of poor communication, lack of forgiveness, holding grudges, forgetting to say thank you, neglecting to pray together. Ask God to show you what little foxes are spoiling your vineyard. Are you feeding some of them? Then pray for the grace to catch them and run them out.

IDOLATRY

Sometimes we allow the idolatries of the world to creep into our hearts and minds. It may be the lies of materialism and the pride of life. You may be making your house or your fitness program or your friendships or your grandchildren into little idols. Root these attitudes out. They are vicious foxes.

A good marriage is a tremendous gift. Steward this gift wisely. Thank God regularly for your husband. Give yourself afresh to your duties of respect and submission. Then you can expect God to prosper your marriage all the way to the end.

Widowhood

Many of us are going to be widows someday, and I know this is not a topic we want to think about, much less plan for. But if we are wise women, we will be considering our ways and planning for possible contingencies. Not worrying. Not fretting. Trusting God. But in the meantime, thanking God for each day with our husbands, and being faithful stewards of the blessings we enjoy.

If you are not a widow, now is a good time to get your husband's counsel on what he would want you to do (with your resources, your home, etc.) if he were to suddenly die. It happens, so a little preparation will go a long way to helping you know how to navigate very difficult circumstances. But even more important than our husband's practical help, we need to know what the Bible says to and about widows.

It is clear that God has a tender spot toward the widow. In fact, He considers visiting orphans and widows in their affliction to be "pure and undefiled religion" (James 1:27). We see three things here. The first is God's acknowledgment that to be a widow is an affliction. It is a hardship that God understands. Second, He knows that the widow can be lonely and needs friends who are looking out for her. And finally, those who are caring for the widow are practicing a pure form of religion, the real gold standard.

Psalm 68:5 identifies God as the judge of the widow, meaning that He looks out for her and protects her. It's surprising how many bad guys will show up to try to take advantage of the widow in her vulnerable state. This was the case in Jesus' day, and it is still the case. But God hates those who do this. Jesus says, "Woe to you, scribes and Pharisees, hypocrites! For you devour widows' houses, and for a pretense make long prayers. Therefore you will receive the greater condemnation" (Matt. 23:14). Those who prey on the widow will receive no mercy from God, but rather greater punishment.

So a widow must seek God's protection, and the church should provide a tangible source of protection for her. One of the duties of the early disciples was to provide for the widows, and because of some kind of ball-drop, seven godly men were appointed to take over this important duty (Acts 6:1–3). So we see God's concern for the widow, one of the most vulnerable members of society.

Now let's turn to Paul's first letter to Timothy which includes some specific instructions about widows. The first thing to note is that there is a category of widows that are "widows indeed." Those are the kind the church is to treat with honor.

1 Timothy 5:3: "Honor widows who are really widows."

So who is really a widow? Who are the women who are most vulnerable and need the church to step in? The ones who have no children or grandchildren.

In his commentary on this passage, Matthew Henry says that "there was in those times an office in the church in which widows were employed, and that was to tend the sick and the aged, to look to them by the direction of the deacons."

So the church provided support for those widows who had no family of their own, who could be "employed" in a sense to help the church. But this was reserved for those widows with specific qualifications.

"But if any widow has children or grandchildren, let them first learn to show piety at home and to repay their parents; for this is good and acceptable before God" (1 Timothy 5:4).

God's design is for children and grandchildren to help their aging parents and grandparents, especially those mothers and grandmothers who have lost their husbands. Paul says this is how children and grandchildren are to learn their religion: by caring for the widows in their family. And notice God's view of this: He calls it good and acceptable for children to "repay their parents" in this way.

So before we move on, note again how God views children caring for their moms and grandmas: He calls it good.

But often today the children are not the problem. It is the widows themselves who might be uncooperative. The "virtue" of our day is independence. Older parents often reject their children's sincere desire to be more helpful. A widow may very much need to receive help from her children, but she refuses. She says she "doesn't want to be a burden." This is our culture's catechism that we are reciting when we say this, and it can make the children's lives far more complicated.

We have to determine that we will be the grateful recipients of their offers of care when the time comes that we actually need it. We don't want to be an affliction to our children, but that can come in more ways than one. If your children are trying to get you to move in with them, be cooperative and tell them you will pray about it. Seek godly counsel. Be humble.

Once a few years ago in the midst of a conversation about a situation of an older woman who was living alone, my son said something like, "Don't worry, Mom, you will be living with us way before that happens." My immediate response was something like, "Oh, no, that won't be necessary." But then (thank the Lord), I said, "Can we please rewind that tape? Thank you, my son."

It is our first impulse to reject the idea that we might ever be so frail or infirm as to need to move in with our children. But we need to get over this. We all know of cases where the children tried to get their parents to move in with them, but they met with stiff resistance. By the time they had to move in, it was much more difficult than it would have been if done earlier.

Now I realize that there can be other reasons for not wanting to move in with your children. But be committed to the Scriptures and recognize that your children have an obligation before God to care for you when you need it. Don't make it harder for them than it needs to be.

A GODLY WIDOW

Sometimes a woman is left with no children or grandchildren to help her, so she may need to be "taken into the number" by the church. How can the church determine who qualifies for such aid? Here it is.

> Do not let a widow under sixty years old be taken into the number, and not unless she has been the wife of one man, well reported for good works: if she has brought up children, if she has lodged strangers, if she has washed the saints' feet, if she has relieved the afflicted, if she has diligently followed every good work. (1 Tim. 5:9–10)

We see here first some very practical qualifications: she must be sixty or older and married only once. But then we turn to look at her reputation for good works. What is this woman known for?

She has been bringing up children, a homemaker, feeding and serving people, caring for those in need, and lots of other good stuff (apparently too many things to list). In other words, she has been a hard-working woman, not self-indulgent, but given to helping others in countless ways over many years.

What disqualifies a widow from being "taken into the number"? If she lives for pleasure. Rather than being given to serving others, this woman is living for herself, entertaining herself, looking for pleasure. That is not good preparation for being of use to the church as a widow. In fact, Paul says that she is as good as dead now, of no use to anyone(v. 6). That is a terrifying description.

The other thing that qualifies her is if she is too young. In this case, she may change her mind about serving the church and remarry. And she may learn to fritter her time away idly, being a busybody on Facebook.

We can take these requirements as good guidelines for our lives now, whether we become widows or not. This is good preparation for whatever lies in our future as women: we are to be busy with children, busy with meals, busy with helping out, not idle, not seeking after our own pleasure, not being a gossip or listening to gossip, but faithfully doing our duties today.

And though God may give us faithful children and grandchildren who will care for us if we are left alone, these duties laid out for faithful widows are basic Christian duties, whether widowed or not.

C H A P T E R   5

The Mother-in-Law

As we look forward to our children growing up and getting married, we have to prepare for a change in our job description. Of course this has been happening gradually all along as our children grew from infants to toddlers to teenagers, but becoming a mother-in-law is a much bigger role change. You will now be in a relationship with a son-in-law or daughter-in-law whom you did not raise. And though it is a wonderful promotion, it requires wisdom to navigate this new role successfully.

What do I mean by "successfully"? Well the stereotypical mother-in-law does not have a very good reputation. What is she noted for? We all know this part of our cultural catechism very well: she is domineering and controlling, critical and opinionated, and pretty much a pain to be around. So the obvious conclusion is "Don't be like that." But the reason the stereotype resonates is because it's not so easy to "not be like that." So we really need help here, and so of course we must look to God's Word for some instructions.

Your son or daughter has married someone from another family, with other family loyalties. This means an entirely different family culture is merging with yours. Your son has chosen a woman who was raised by a different mother, and she has a whole life-time of experiences, training, family relationships, stories, ways of celebrating Christmas and birthdays. Your daughter has been given in marriage, and she has taken another name. Her household is a new creation, not identical to yours. There is a transformation taking place, and it is wonderful to behold. You are called to honor and respect these new covenant households. As a mother and mother-in-law, your duties have changed dramatically. You are no longer responsible in the same way that you were. Your son or son-in-law has taken on new responsibilities; your daughter or daughter-in-law is now under someone else's authority. If we really believe this, if we really have a high view of the family as God created it, then we will live and act as though we believe it.

It turns out that we have an excellent example of a mother-in-law in the Bible, Naomi, Ruth's mother-in-law. Naomi is a widow with two childless daughters-in-law. Naomi is not a likely candidate to be a major figure in the messianic line or to be a main character in a book in the canon of Scripture. But God loves to use unlikely people to tell His story.

LOYALTY BEGETS LOYALTY

> And Naomi said unto her two daughters in law, "Go, return each to her mother's house. The LORD deal kindly with you, as you have dealt with the dead and with me. The LORD grant that you may find rest, each in the house of her husband." So she kissed them, and they lifted up their voices and wept. (Ruth 1:8–9)

Before we look at Ruth's famous response, let's identify four aspects of Naomi's speech.

1. She gives precedence to her daughters-in-law's primary loyalties to their own mothers.
2. She reminds them of the kindness she has received from them. This in itself is kindness.
3. She prays that God will bless them with future homes.
4. She releases them from any obligation to her.
5. She kisses them with warm affection.

Look at the verbs in the list above: gives, reminds,
prays, releases, kisses. This displays Naomi's noble
character. She has nothing to offer her daughters-in-
law, and she knows it. No doubt she would enjoy
the comfort of their companionship and friendship
during this time of heavy loss, but she is thinking of
their future and not her own. She doesn't want them
to be under any obligation to be tied down with her
in a dead-end future. She is loyal to them, and she
honors their loyalties. She wants what is best for
them, and she sets them free.

Now look at Ruth's famous response in verses 16
and 17:

> Entreat me not to leave you, or to turn back from
> following you; for wherever you go, I will go; and
> wherever you lodge, I will lodge; Your people shall
> be my people, and your God, my God. Where you
> die, I will die, and there will I be buried. The LORD
> do so to me, and more also, if anything but death
> parts you and me.

What a response! Ruth has fully identified with her
dead husband's family and faith, and for her, there is
no turning back. Naomi has set her free, and Ruth has
freely made her choice. You can see here how Naomi's
loyalty to God and to Ruth has begotten Ruth's loyalty
to God and to Naomi. It's a beautiful picture.

Now let's go through these five traits of Naomi's and consider how they apply to us. Remember, the mother-in-law has a bad reputation, so in some ways we are already behind the eight ball. In other words, this may not be as easy as we think.

GIVE PRECEDENCE

Loyalties shift. Naomi understood this. When children are growing up, their loyalty should be to their own family. But when a son or daughter marries, this primary loyalty must shift to someone else. This is how is should be. In fact, when it doesn't shift, something is very wrong.

Consider the case of the son who marries. If his mother becomes jealous of the new bride (and all the attention he is lavishing on her), or if the new bride becomes jealous of her mother-in-law (because her new husband hugs his mom whenever he sees her), something is haywire.

We have to remember Naomi. She understood the primary loyalty of each daughter-in-law was to her own mother. Your daughter-in-law is probably closer to her own mother than she is to you. Not always, as seen in Ruth's case, but typically, that is how it is. Maybe your daughter-in-law invites her mother to come help after the baby is born, and she doesn't invite you. Maybe she takes more pictures of the new baby with her own parents than with you. This is all natural and normal, and you cannot succumb to comparisons, jealousies, envy, or resentment because it will only sour things between you.

Actually, loyalty is a wonderful thing. Be thankful for it. How do you want your own daughter or son to treat you? That is how you should want your daughter-in-law or son-in-law to treat their own parents. Don't jostle for position. Don't crowd. Don't be clamoring for it to be your turn. Rather, be thankful.

KINDNESS AND BLESSING

There's really no end to kindness, but here are a couple of ways to extend it to your in-law children. Like Naomi, remind them of their kindness to you. This is always better than criticism and disapproval. I guarantee that if you want to chase your children away, there is no better way to do it than by criticizing them.

Criticism can come in many forms. It can be a raised eyebrow or it can be a snicker or it can be framed as a question or it can be delivered straight. All are lethal. Your married children are grown ups. You had your chance. If you don't like what you see, if you have concerns, take them to God. Pray for them. And wait until you are asked before you give your opinion.

This can be very difficult, particularly if you think they are not making right choices about parenting or finances or job choices or schooling. If they think you are disapproving, they will distance themselves. Why? Because your disapproval hurts. They want your approval and your encouragement. Where there is love and acceptance, they will move in closer. My husband describes criticism as chasing your kids away with a stick. And then we wonder why they don't want to be with us!

Now I am certainly not suggesting that you manipulate by lying. That would be ludicrous. What I mean is that you focus on the good things that you see. Naomi reminded her daughters-in-law of their kindness to her. So think about those things and thank you own daughter-in-law or son-in-law for their kindness to you.

If you don't see anything good, then you may have allowed a critical spirit to take root. Weed that out first, and then begin to be positive. Give them room. Reminder: you are not the Holy Spirit. Be flexible and kind-hearted.

SET THEM FREE

Do not load your married children and in-law children with expectations. God is writing their story, not you. When you get your hands off the pencil, you will have more fun and so will they. When you set them free from all your own needs and expectations, your relationship will prosper. Setting them free means deferring to their schedule, their preferences, their own family culture and customs, their own decisions. Nothing will alienate you quicker than criticism.

Some of you may be saying, "Ouch!" If you are, then think for a minute about how you felt when you got married. Did you want your parents hovering over you, or complaining about the way you were doing things? Did they insist you spend Thanksgiving with them because you spent last Thanksgiving with the other in-laws? That's a terrible burden to put on your kids. Set them free to spend Christmas where and when they want. Yes, invite them. But let them know you are fine with whatever they want to do. No pressure. No strings. That's what it means to set them free.

Here's an example. Let's say you home-schooled your children, but now they have decided to enroll their children in a Christian day school. Don't take this personally. This is so important. Don't be negative. Rather, think about how you can contribute toward tuition or school uniforms. It's so easy to be negative. It requires thoughtfulness to be positive. Use your tongue to build up, to encourage, to praise.

But what if you set them free and they move across the country or out of the country? Then be loyal. Visit often. Call. Send gifts to the kids. Be their biggest fan.

AFFECTION

Be warm and affectionate to your in-law children. That may look different with each one, but figure it out and be demonstrative. Naomi kissed her daughters-in-law as she sent them away. We see how affectionate she was toward them. She didn't pretend. She was committed to each one and loved each one. Even though Orpah kissed Naomi goodbye and chose to go back to her own mother, there is no indication that Naomi was hurt by this. Rather, she urged Ruth to follow her sister-in-law's example.

The way to show affection varies. It might look like a hug or simply a big welcoming smile. It can include asking about work or about the kids, making a cup of coffee, sharing meals, babysitting, giving gifts, opening your home. When you feel your heart drawing back, confess it to God. Ask for more affection and kindness, and then bestow it. God will bless it.

NO FAVORITES

Just one more thing before we look at another mother-in-law. Notice that Naomi doesn't play favorites with her daughters-in-law. She treats them both the same. She doesn't say, "Orpah, I think Ruth and I will get along better, so you feel free to go back to your mother." She sets both young women free, and there is no indication that the relationship is lop-sided. A mother-in-law needs to be careful to treat all her children and in-law children with the same affection. Playing favorites is not wise. At the same time, getting along with one better than another does not equal having a favorite. If you play favorites, you are setting your children up for competition, envy, and jealousy. If you are wise, you will steer clear of this.

ANOTHER MOTHER-IN-LAW

Now let's look at another mother-in-law in the Scriptures, this time in the New Testament.

"Now when Jesus had come into Peter's house, He saw his wife's mother lying sick with a fever. So He touched her hand, and the fever left her. And she arose and served them" (Mt. 8:14–15).

Peter's mother-in-law was sick, and Jesus healed her with a touch of His hand. But notice what she did upon rising from her bed. She got up and served. She didn't rise up to be served, nor did anyone suggest she get back to work. She was self-motivated and freely oriented toward service to others.

SERVICE WITHOUT STRINGS

We women are naturally good at service and support. Like Peter's mother-in-law, we know what it means to bestow much labor on our husbands, our kids, our grandkids, our friends, and the church. In fact, that is the order I think it should fall in. We should start with our own family and move outward. But there can be a snare even in the best kind of serving, and that is when it is more about us than about them.

If we are attempting to use our service to make us feel needed, it will suck all the life and good out of all we do. In other words, there is a certain kind of service that has strings, that seeks to gratify the flesh, that is more of an affliction to others than a blessing. And unfortunately, it is obvious to the recipient. This is the kind of service that becomes more of an harassment than a blessing to our kids.

How does this happen? It happens when we are serving because we want some thanks and appreciation. It happens when we are keeping track of how much we have given and how much we have received. It happens when we are looking for reciprocity, so we are giving to get. In other words, it happens when it's more about us than about them.

When we give freely, we are a tremendous resource of motherly affection, support, attention, loyalty, and blessing.

So what is the conclusion? Set them free! Don't chase them away with a stick. Imitate Naomi. Her covenant faithfulness resulted in great blessing.

In Ruth 4:14–15, after the birth of Obed, the women said to Naomi, "Blessed be the Lord who has not left you this day without a close relative; and may his name be famous in Israel! And may he be to you a restorer of life and a nourisher of your old age; for your daughter-in-law, who loves you, who is better to you than seven sons, has borne him."

CHAPTER 6

The Glory of Grandmothers

N ow here is a topic we are all fond of discussing: the joy of being a grandmother! Even though I have been a grandma now for almost twenty years, it is still a delight to be with my grandchildren, to talk about my grandchildren, and to ponder the mystery of this blessing of children's children.

When my daughter Bekah was expecting our first grandchild, I was so excited that I made a point of visiting with some of the godly older women in our community who were experienced grandmas. I still remember the joy they had in sharing some of their insights with me. Each one spoke with fondness and pride of her grandchildren, and each shared her ideas and experiences with me on how to be a blessing as well as a blessed grandma. And so, when our first grandson, Knox, arrived, it was a thrilling event. And each one since (six more boys and ten girls) has added more to the total tonnage of joy and blessings in our family.

With blessing, of course, comes responsibility. As one of my children once pointed out, a basket of fruit is heavy. And as God as added more and more, it requires more strength and stamina for us to carry it. And fruit is messy too. But who would dream of forgoing the enjoyment of the fruit to avoid having to wipe up a mess? Believe me, I will take the mess any day.

God's Covenant Blessings

Even though most people in the world agree that grandchildren are one of the sweetest blessings, we still need to anchor this experiential knowledge to God's Word. Children's children are a sign of His blessing. They are not just a random blessing bestowed on us, the "lucky" grandparents.

"The Lord bless you out of Zion, and may you see the good of Jerusalem all the days of your life. Yes, may you see your children's children. Peace be upon Israel!" (Ps. 128:5–6).

"But the mercy of the Lord is from everlasting to everlasting on those who fear Him, and His righteousness to children's children, to such as keep His covenant, and to those who remember His commandments to do them" (Ps. 103:17–18).

"Children's children are the crown of old men, and the glory of children is their father" (Prov. 17:6).

Seeing our grandchildren is seeing the good of Jerusalem. When we have godly grandchildren preparing to take our place in this world, this is God's great mercy to us. We are handing them the baton. And when Doug and I go, we are handing the baton off to a battalion of seventeen!

But notice a very important point in Psalm 103. This blessing of mercy and righteousness is conditional. It is not automatic. It is for those who fear God and keep His covenant and His commandments. We are required to be faithful if we want covenant blessings for our children and grandchildren. And as we walk in obedience, we must trust God for faithful descendants. If we forget his commandments and do not keep covenant, then we cannot expect mercy and righteousness for our children and grandchildren. This is a very serious matter.

But when we do remember and fear God, He sends peace. Peace be upon Israel. His mercy and righteousness is ongoing, from one generation to the next and the next and the next, from everlasting to everlasting. We have the privilege of being part of this chain of covenant blessing, and we want to extend the blessings that preceded us to the blessings that follow behind us. This is the most important duty of grand-parenting. I know when I talk about this, I am talking about something that is way over my head. But even though I don't understand the depths of the wisdom of God and His unsearchable judgments, I know that our grandchildren are our crown and glory.

GOD'S COVENANT PROMISES

God's promises concerning generational faithfulness are all tied up with our grandchildren. As we see in the verses cited above, our children's children are our glory and crown. And just as a crown sets a queen apart, so our grandchildren set us apart.

One summer a few years ago we had an elderly woman named Bertha from Maya, Mexico, (who couldn't speak English) at our table for Sabbath dinner. Her granddaughter Grace was moving in with us while she attended New St. Andrews College. This little lady (under five feet tall) in her upper eighties was a little unsure about leaving her granddaughter in northern Idaho, and so I took the opportunity to start introducing her to my grandchildren.

We were eating outside in the yard, and as the grandkids finished dinner, they got up to run around and play. I snagged them one at a time as they ran past my chair, and I introduced them to Berta. Her face lit up each time as I told her their name and as they greeted her. After I got to a dozen or so, she became incredulous! Grace interpreted for me, and her grandmother told me I was a queen! I will never forget it. All those beautiful grandchildren added up to a very large crown in her eyes.

And so I am a queen, and so are you if you have a crown of grandchildren—which you can only have if you are a crown to them as well. This goes back to the earlier chapters where we discussed who we are in Christ and how we are commissioned as older women to live in a manner that brings glory to Him. With a crown comes the responsibility to wear it well, to live worthy of this crown of blessings. This leads nicely into the next chapter where I want to deal with the duties of the grandma. But before we do that, I want to look a bit more closely at Proverbs 17:6.

"Children's children are the crown of old men, and the glory of children is their father."

You might wonder how I get a crown for grandma out of a "crown of old men"? And if the glory of children is their father, then why am I applying that to grandmas? These are great questions, and you'll have to bear with me as I try to explain how I get there. Language starts to fail as we consider glory and a crown.

If we back up a minute, we'll remember that a virtuous wife is the crown of her husband. So I am my husband's crown, his first crown, and he is the glory of our children. So that makes me, in a sense, the crown of the glory. It's as if the glory gets more potent when it is crowned, or the crown is more magnificent when it sits on a glory. And this is just describing parents, and not grandparents.

But with grandchildren it gets even more glorious. If my husband is the glory of our kids (and he is), and if I am his crown (the glory of this glory, the crown of his crown), and if he is now wearing a crown of grandchildren to top it all off, do you see how it is building glory upon glory upon glory, crown upon crown upon crown? So in a sense, the grandchildren are crowning my crown (again).

The crown is a metaphor, but this is also a reality. Being a crown is being an adornment. We set off, display, and magnify what or who we crown. So a grandmother, in a sense, is a queen with a beautiful crown who magnifies her husband, children, and grandchildren. What does that mean exactly? We make them all look good.

"For the LORD is good; His mercy is everlasting, and His truth endures to all generations" (Ps. 100:5).

CHAPTER 7

The Duties of the Grandma

We are all pretty familiar with the delights of being someone's grandma, but are there any serious duties associated with this "office"? Yes indeed there are. Just as a mother-in-law is called to loyalty and service and support, these same duties characterize the faithful grandmother as well.

MODEL FAITHFULNESS.

If we want grandchildren who will remember His commandments and keep His covenant, then we must be actively engaged in doing this ourselves. This means we will model faithfulness. We must give our grandchildren a living picture of what means to live in and love God's covenant.

PRAY FOR THEM.

Our first duty is to trust God for our grandchildren and pray for them to walk in the covenant all their days. Because Doug and I have so many grandkids, we have made prayer cards for them so we can pray specifically for one each day. While we are at it, we pray for their future spouses, too.

TEACH THEM TO FEAR THE LORD.

"Only take heed to yourself and diligently keep yourself, lest you forget the things your eyes have seen, and lest they depart from your heart all the days of your life. And teach them to your children and your grandchildren" (Deut. 4:9).

Sometimes your teaching will be hands on, and sometimes it will be from a distance. Take what opportunities you have and make the most of them. If you are helping home-school your grandchildren, for example, you will have some clear-cut opportunities to do some direct teaching. Just as parents are called to teach their children while they walk along the way, your interaction with your grandchildren, whether in the car or at your table, should always be in acknowledgment of God's faithfulness and goodness. This doesn't mean you only talk to them about the Bible. But you want them to see you living out what you say you believe.

If you are at a distance, there are many ways to connect with your grandchildren today. I still have letters that I wrote to my grandma when I was eight and nine years old. For some reason, she saved these and my mother passed them on to me. What this tells me is that my handwritten letters were very precious to her. But it was my mother who encouraged me to write to her, and my grandma always wrote back. Today, with skype and texting and email, we have so many ways to visit with our people that it's not really necessary to write a letter with pen and paper. But I still recommend it. Write your grandkids. Send them postcards when you travel.

Grandma Lois

I thank God, whom I serve with a pure conscience, as my forefathers did, as without ceasing I remember you in my prayers night and day, greatly desiring to see you, being mindful of your tears, that I may be filled with joy, when I call to remembrance the genuine faith that is in you, which dwelt first in your grandmother Lois and your mother Eunice, and I am persuaded is in you also. (2 Tim. 1:3–5)

> But you must continue in the things which you have
> learned and been assured of, knowing from whom
> you have learned them, and that from childhood
> you have known the Holy Scriptures, which are
> able to make you wise for salvation through faith
> which is in Christ Jesus. (2 Tim. 3:14–15)

How would you like to be the kind of grandma who made it into the New Testament? Grandma Lois had an impressive influence on her grandson Timothy, as Paul points out here in his second letter to the young man. Lois had "genuine faith," and she and Eunice were responsible for making Timothy well acquainted with the Scriptures as a child. We can pray that we will have a similar impact on our own grandchildren. Our responsibility is to faithfully transmit all we can of God's goodness to them every chance we get. God will use it all as He sees fit.

TELL THEM STORIES.
One of the wonderful opportunities you have open to you is storytelling. Tell your grandchildren the stories of God's faithfulness to you and your family in the past. My grandchildren love to hear about my childhood and their parents' childhood. Two of my older grandsons visit their great-grandfather

every Saturday. It started out with him teaching them on evangelism, but he intersperses it all with stories of his life. What an opportunity for them! A few years ago my son spent a whole weekend recording my father telling stories. Now that he has passed, we are all the more grateful that we have those stories recorded.

Every family has stories, and we have some favorites. One of the all-time favorites involves my husband Douglas when he was four or five years old. His father had recently left the US Navy and was working for a Christian ministry, so the funds were short and their faith was a little shaky now that they could no longer count on a monthly paycheck. They had three little kids, and they were out of bread and milk, so they called a family prayer meeting and asked Doug (being the oldest) to pray. They thought that he could probably pray with more faith. So he did. He prayed for milk and bread. Within moments of praying, the doorbell rang, and a milkman stood at the door congratulating them for having won a year's supply of milk! Now we have four generations who treasure this story of God's extravagant kindness. I am confident our grandchildren will someday be telling their own children and grandchildren this story. These stories are part of their inheritance.

SING SOME SONGS!

Each family culture has some songs that have been handed down and songs that are new to the family. Songs are another part of what you are handing down to your grandchildren, so do some singing.

Because my husband plays the guitar, he sang to our kids when they were little, and he has sung for years to our grandkids. He sings them silly songs when they are little, making up songs about them "walking the plank" as they jump off our hearth to the tune of "What do you do with a scurvy pirate?" He has written a silly verse for each child, and it is a great favorite which they have all loved in their turn. As they outgrow these songs, we move on to other kinds of singing.They also know many Scripture songs, and we sing them when we get together.

This is another part of the joy we are inviting our grandchildren into when we welcome them into our home. This is part of their spiritual inheritance. So be generous with your time, your attention, your stories, and your songs.

LEAVE AN INHERITANCE.

"A good man leaves an inheritance to his children's children, but the wealth of the sinner is stored up for the righteous" (Prov. 13:22).

Of course we understand that a spiritual inheritance is of more value than a physical inheritance, but Proverbs says it is good to leave a real tangible inheritance to your children's children. It is never too soon to be thinking about this. Some of this inheritance may be in the form of stuff rather than money, so we should consider our inventory and be thinking about what we are going to be leaving our grandchildren.

I am of the opinion that we ought to give as much as we can to our grandchildren while we are living, and by this I mean passing things on that they will appreciate while we can still tell them the back story. For example, my great-grandmother Mae Downing was known for her quilts, and my mom passed one on to me some years ago. It had been well used, so it was not in pristine condition, but all the little scraps of cloth were sewn together by hand in such a lovely pattern. I have already given this quilt to my granddaughter Evangeline Mae, and her mother has tucked it away for her. How much better to tell the story of my great-grandma in person to my granddaughter, than to have my children find a quilt in the attic after I am gone and wonder who made it and where it came from. Instead, Evangeline has a little something from her great-great-great grandmother, for whom she was named.

Every family has stories and keepsakes of various kinds to pass down, and I don't believe we should burden our children and grandchildren with boxes of memorabilia that mean nothing to them. Nor should we be setting our grandchildren up to be eyeing our stuff and wondering what they will be getting from us. This requires wisdom. Fit the inheritance to the grandchild and be evenhanded. And make certain you have put things in writing.

The reason I care about handing off rings and necklaces and quilts and china to my children and grandchildren is because I love God's covenant. These things are earthly reminders to us of God's faithfulness over generations. The bed downstairs belonged to my grandchildren's Great-Great-Great Grandma Hattie. That's a five-generation hand off.

When we give, we should give with absolutely no strings. If we hand off great-grandma's velvet settee, we should not flip out if we hear that it was auctioned off or painted red. Remember, it is just stuff, and if it is not meaningful to our kids, then they should feel free to either give it to one of the other children who will appreciate it, or get rid of it.

We each have unique circumstances that will govern what kind and how much of an inheritance we can leave for our children and grandchildren. Given our resources, we should find the best way to save for them. Maybe you are saving for them by paying off your mortgage. Perhaps you have started a savings account for each one. The principle is to have them in mind. You've probably seen the bumper sticker on the back of a large RV that says, "I'm spending my children's inheritance." This is funny, but not funny. We should be deliberate about what we are setting aside for them, remembering that this is good in God's sight.

GIVE GIFTS.

As I write this, I am already gathering Christmas gifts for my seventeen grandchildren. This is a big commitment, so I need to get started as soon as possible, and not the week before Christmas. My husband and I have made gift-giving part of the household budget. With so many of us now, each month has a birthday or two (or three) to celebrate. So we may as well plan intelligently for this!

The thing we grandmas need to remember is to give our gifts in line with what their parents want them to have. If they don't want their kids to have puzzles, then of course don't give them puzzles. Or loud toys. Or expensive dolls. If they don't want their kids to have candy, don't sneak them candy. We may not agree with the parents' decision, but they are the parents, and it is not worth having a collision over such things. My mother-in-law found it difficult to get out and shop, and she had no idea what to buy for our kids, so she would give me a check each Christmas with a designated amount for each child. Then she asked me to shop for them, give her the gift, and she would wrap it and give it to them. This worked well for both of us.

One thing I would advise you in this business of gift-giving: don't start what you can't finish. If you decide, for example, to fill a stocking for each grandchild at Christmas, you have to see it through to the finish line. So think about this before you get started.

As I've mentioned, I have seventeen grandkids now, so filling those Christmas stockings is no small thing. About five years into it, I started to think about backing out, hoping no one would notice. But someone did. My oldest grandson, who was about five years old, asked me, "Nana, are you doing stockings for us this year?" What could I do but say, "Of course I am, Knox!" And so I have been filling stockings ever since. My children have told me that the grandkids look forward to this, even the older ones, so I press on to the finish line. No backing out!

BE SUPPORTIVE.

We can't always predict how we will be used to bless our children and grandchildren. But we can look for our opportunities and fit them to our resources of time and money. Our goal should be to reinforce our children's good example in teaching their own children. We are not the parents, so we should not try to steer. In all these things we should defer to the parents; they have been placed in authority over these children, and we have not. If we want to be a blessing to our children and grandchildren, we will remember this.

"Children's children are the crown of old men, and the glory of children is their father" (Prov. 17:6). God has given our grandchildren parents who are their glory. We should do all we can, given the context and the story they are in, to reinforce this. And then we can be content to enjoy being the crown!

FEED THEM.

Food is a tremendous and tangible gift that you can bestow on your grandchildren when they come in your door. Feed them! This is such an enormous topic that I am going to devote the following chapter to it, so I will simply list it here and move on.

CHAPTER 8

Common Temptations

With all the joys and benefits of being a mother-in-law and a grandma, you can expect that temptations will come. The enemy always wants to sow discord, particularly in the closest of relationships. Our goal in raising our children is to equip them to be parents and grandparents themselves, so we want to cheer them on as they grow into new responsibilities. How sad to allow sin to get in the way of enjoying the best years and the sweetest relationships of our lives! We can't just drift along and hope all will go well. We have to be intentional about doing good and vigilant to

resist those common temptations and ungodly attitudes that will destroy the unity and joy we have
in Christ.

A CRITICAL SPIRIT

The first all-purpose relationship destroyer is criticism. You know you have a critical spirit when you
see all the shortcomings so clearly. It is only made
worse when you meditate on those shortcomings.
This will essentially train you to have an even sharper
eye to spot more defects. And so the tendency grows.

You cannot suppose that there will be never be anything in your children, their marriages, or your own
precious grandchildren that you could possibly find
fault with. Of course there will be many such things.
So we must be disposed to deal with these things and
not be surprised by them. Fault-finding is the easiest
thing in the world. There is no skill involved in this.
Seeing the fault is not the sin. It is dwelling on it, being
hurt by it, and feeling offended that are fleshly, natural, and prideful responses. On the other hand, over-
looking and over-loving the faults we see in others is
a remarkable sign of grace. That is what we want.

Proverbs 19:11 says, "The discretion of a man makes
him slow to anger, and his glory is to overlook a
transgression." Transgressions will come, both sins
of omission and sins of commission. What kinds of

sins of omission? Forgetting to say thank you, neglecting to listen, failing to respond to your emails, ignoring your requests. Sins of commission? Oh, there are plenty of opportunities for provocation in this world!

Have you ever thought about how much your own parents had to overlook in you? Now that I am a grandma myself, I see my own mother's sweetness and kindness with new eyes. There was so much she could have criticized, but she didn't. She blessed me in countless sacrificial ways, and I was often thoughtless. On the other hand, if I felt criticized by my parents or in-laws in the choices my husband and I were making, it always put a strain on our relationship with them.

When we are criticized, our natural instinct is to become defensive and draw back, even if the criticism is true. So don't put your children on the defensive. If you see something imperfect, overlook it and press on. If it is serious enough to bring it up with them, pray over it for a few days and then pray for an opportunity to address it. But that should be very uncommon. Most of our fault-finding is nickle-and-dime stuff that should be covered in love. "Hatred stirs up strife, but love covers all sins" (Prov. 10:12).

Criticisms come in many forms. You might be critical of the parenting style of your son-in-law or daughter-in-law and differ over many things, great and small. The big things might include their choices of education or how they discipline (or don't discipline). Or it might be small things, like how many blankets the baby should be wrapped in. Constant "input" with a critical edge will cause your children to move out of range.

Criticism kills. It makes your children feel they are always being evaluated and judged (because they are), and it certainly does not build them up. The solution is to find things to praise them and thank them for. Rather than killing the relationship with criticism, kill the criticism with kindness and love.

CORRECTION

Correcting the children when their parents are in the room is not a good idea. Of course, if they are just about to step into the fire, grab them! But telling them to be nice to their siblings or to sit up straight at the table when Mom and Dad are right there is out of line. It is not your call, it is not your problem, it is not your jurisdiction. If you are babysitting, discuss ahead of time how the parents want you to handle correction. But stay out of the way when they are back on duty.

My daughter Rachel has a great system that has worked well when I babysit her children. She tells the children that if they disobey their Nana while she is gone, I will put a black spot on the back of their hand. Then when she gets back, she will deal with the black spot. This has worked beautifully. If a little one starts to wander into a little disobedience, I simply have to remind him or her of the potential black spot, and there is quick compliance. I think I may have only had to give one black spot, but I'm not even sure if I remember that right. It's been an effective method.

Now, if the black spot method didn't work, and the children were naughty and disobedient, this would affect how often I would want to babysit. But because they are well behaved and delightful children, it is a joy to help out in this way.

I do not spank the grandkids. If they need discipline, I will tell their parents when they pick them up, and the parents can deal with it. So, we grandmas are not in authority over the grandchildren, and we are certainly not in authority over their parents either. We had our chance! It is not our place to correct our children. We are to encourage and respect them, not scold them.

COMPLAINING

I guarantee if you complain to the kids about their parents or complain to the parents about the kids, they will get more and more distant. The same goes for complaining to one of your grown children about the other. It is far more pleasant to speak of their good qualities than to complain about the bad ones.

Don't complain about how little you see the grandkids. Don't complain about how long it's been since you've had a visit. Don't complain about your daughter's housekeeping or your son-in-law's forgetfulness or your grandkids' tardiness or anything else. We are far more likely to cut ourselves slack than to extend it to others. Rather than complaining, offer to help, laugh off their forgetfulness, overlook their tardiness. We've *all* been tardy and forgetful.

Basically, let's all act like Christians!

COMPARISONS

My mother-in-law was famous for saying, "Comparisons are odious." And so they are. I mentioned this in the chapter on mother-in-laws, but it bears mentioning again. Never compare the amount of time you get with the grandkids to the amount the other set of grandparents get. Focus instead on making *your* time with them sweeter and sweeter. This is not a competition.

Comparisons will transform what was once a fun visit into an obligation and a minefield. Your children will be tip-toeing through each visit trying to get to the finish line with no injury. Comparisons are total kill-joys. They hurt and separate and turn everything into a competition.

Here's an example. If you make a pie for Thanksgiving, and your son-in-law says good, but not quite as good as his mom's, you probably won't be flattered. Neither will your daughter-in-law if you compare her pie to your daughter's. You get the picture. The only fruit from such comments is a bitter fruit. It makes no sense to live this way. Life is too short. Fill your visits with gratitude and don't compare.

SMOTHERING AND SPOILING

A grandma who spoils and smothers is deadly. We want grandchildren to grow up to be faithful Christians, courageous and strong, who will contend with their enemies in the gate, not pampered and self-centered cowards. This should be our prayer!

This means we will not be the grandma who never says no to little Johnny, or thinks he never needs correction from his parents, or slips him candy when his mama isn't looking, or thinks every bump should be a visit to the ER. This kind of grandma will either drive all her grandkids far away or will cause them to think of her as a vending machine.

If you spend too much money on the grandkids in unwise ways, they will not prosper. Be wise. Be a blessing. Don't smother them with too much affection and don't spoil them with too much stuff. They do not live to meet your need to be needed. Don't try to buy their affection with gifts.

Go ahead and bestow on the grandkids at birthdays and Christmas, but only in ways the parents will appreciate and not dread. I have talked with mothers who find Christmas gifts from Grandma to be a problem to navigate and not a blessing to enjoy. Let's say Grandma sends the twelve-year-old grandson a Winnie the Pooh sweatshirt, and then expects to see him wearing it when he would rather be dead in a ditch. Or let's say the parents do not want the kids playing video games, so Grandma sends a stack of them for Christmas. You get the idea.

Parents do not appreciate interference when they are running the game. If a child is being corrected, this is not the time to speak up on the child's defense and tell the parents they are being too hard. This is another set up for resentment and misunderstanding to grow. Pray for the parents to be wise, and thank God for them. Of course, this is assuming the parents are not being crazy, yelling or hitting or otherwise exhibiting ungodly behavior. If that is happening, I am not telling you to sit meekly by.

SENTIMENTALISM

This is related to smothering and spoiling. Sentimentalism is thinking of our grandkids in an emotional haze and looking for them to make our life complete in some way. If we are expecting each relationship to be rainbows and lollipops, then we are not thinking biblically.

We are right to have deep loyalty and affection for our children's children. But they have their own lives, and Grandma is not in the center of it, nor should she be. We are to be content to be a source of joy and blessing, not *the* source of joy and blessing. We are on the sidelines, cheering them on, not coaching them.

Sentimentalism is when we are looking for an particular feeling and wanting to call it up on demand. Faithfulness is when we are doing what is right, regardless of how we feel. Though feelings are wonderful, we don't serve them. We serve God and He blesses us with joy.

Serious Disagreements

What about when we legitimately disagree with our children? What then?

Let's run a couple of scenarios where you might disagree. Your son-in-law decides they are no longer going to celebrate Christmas. This is sad, but it is not breaking God's law. We are not required to celebrate Christmas. You should honor their request to send no gifts. Pray for them, and look for other times you can celebrate with them.

Let's say they are sending their kids off to a boarding school. Don't be hasty and react or over-react. You can certainly ask questions and pray for opportunities to discuss your concerns. You can even let them know that you cannot bless their decision, but you can continue to be kind and loving. If you break fellowship over such things, you will cut off any opportunity to bless your grandkids, and they may need it more than ever.

In all serious disagreements, the goal should be to keep the peace and preserve the unity. They might be making a foolish decision. If that is the case, God will not bless it. But if you cut them off, you will not be there to help them when they realize they've messed up. God is sanctifying them. He is writing their story, and He is not finished yet. Act wisely, and don't burn your bridges.

If the church excommunicates one of your children for misbehavior, this does not mean you have to excommunicate them from your life. It may be serious enough that you remove them from your will. It may be that you have to set conditions on when you will see them and how you will see them. But you should continue to pray for them and seek them out like a shepherd seeking a lost sheep.

Christianity is lived out in our relationships, and obedience is not always easy. But it is always fruitful.

CHAPTER 9

Feed Your People

"**G**o, eat your bread with joy, and drink your wine with a merry heart" (Ecclesiastes 9:7).

If you were going to ask me what I think the most important thing we do for our grandchildren is, I would not have to think twice about it. The answer is Sabbath Dinner.

Like the traditional Sunday Dinner, our Sabbath Dinner is a weekly celebration where we all sit down together and share a meal. We decided twenty years ago that rather than eating after church on Sunday, we would gather on Saturday night at 6 pm as a kick-off to the Lord's Day. And we've been doing this ever since.

THE GUEST LIST

Our children and grandchildren come, as well as my in-law children's families who live in town. This means our regular crew includes my son-in-law's mother, my daughter-in-law's brother and his wife and family, and my other son-in-law's brother. And of course my eighty-nine-year-old father-in-law joins us as well. And the four college students who live with us. Not to scare you off, but this means that if everyone comes, our regular weekly number for dinner is thirty-five. And usually we have out-of-town guests, so the number can easily reach forty-five.

The other thing that has happened is the presence of strangers. We regularly have people visiting Moscow, visiting the church, visiting NSA, or visiting Logos School who end up at our Sabbath Dinner. This is such a delight to us. Our children feel free to invite these folks to come (or we do if we meet them first), and I look forward to the day when my grandchildren start bringing friends, which has only happened a couple of times so far.

DINING ROOM DILEMMAS

Let me assure you of two things. First, when we started, there were just six of us, and God has graciously added to our number slowly. It has taken us twenty years to get to this size. So I learned how to double and triple and quadruple recipes gradually. Not only that, but I added to the cooking and dining supplies gradually as well. Second, I do not have a huge dining room. In fact, I have had visitors ask me (after seeing my dining room) where I serve Sabbath Dinner. The answer is that I serve it all over the house, wherever you can find a seat!

My cooking is not amazing and my house is not amazing. The amazing thing is that people want to come. But they are not coming for the food only. They are coming because they love to be together. The cousins are always happy to see each other, and the adults look forward to relaxing, having a glass of wine, and visiting.

No pressure

From the very beginning, our Sabbath Dinner has been a "get to" not a "got to" affair. We have been careful not to put any burden of obligation on our children, and from time to time we have reminded them that they are free to come or not come. But they assure me this is not necessary. They want to come!

Sabbath Dinner is an important part of the weekly rhythm, and when we are out of town or when it is canceled due to a schedule conflict, it throws us all off. It really has become an anchor for the week. And next to worship, we view it as the most important thing we do. It is a well-established tradition at our house. The older grandchildren hate to miss it as much as the little ones. It is our time to recalibrate, catch up, laugh together, make plans, and enjoy each other.

WHO DOES THE DISHES?

The bigger our Sabbath Dinner has grown, the more the help has grown along with it. Sometimes a couple of grandkids will come over Saturday late afternoon to help me set up. Families contribute to the food and the wine. Clean-up happens without me orchestrating it. If our children were not participating in this way, Doug and I might collapse under the weight of it all. But they are hands on and hands in. This is because they have taken ownership of our Sabbath Dinner. It is not something "that Mom and Dad do" but it is something we all do together.

Every family should be celebrating the Lord's Day together, and there is no need to wait until you have grandchildren. You may decide to make it a weekly brunch after church, a full Sunday Dinner with china and crystal, or a Sabbath Dinner on Saturday night like ours. We have made a long-term investment (of time, money, and trouble) that has already paid incredible returns. God has blessed it far beyond what I could have expected or imagined.

THE NITTY GRITTY

Now to anticipate a few questions. No, I don't use fancy china. I have a stack of simple white buffet plates and a stack of lightweight Corelle (which is my favorite). I often use disposable plates for the younger kids' table, and when we are outside in the summer, I sometimes use disposable for everyone. But since the adults usually sit around in the living room and not at a table, it's more helpful for them to have an actual plate.

When we were a smaller number, we could fit around my 18–foot table and pass the food family style. But now we use a buffet most all the time. We usually serve the younger kids at the table first, then the older kids and the adults go through the buffet line. (It's getting harder and harder to tell the older grandkids and the adults apart!) I often set up a table in the library for the older kids. And sometimes we push the living room furniture around to accommodate folding tables for the adults. It just depends on the week.

I use canvas drop cloths on my six-foot folding tables. They are a great neutral color, wash up well, and I can bleach them to get out any stains. (You can get these at a hardware store and they are not expensive.) I do put candles and flowers on the tables, but they are often what I pick out of my garden and nothing fancy.

The menu is as simple as I can make it because I will be making a pretty large quantity. In other words, complicated recipes are not what I look for when I'm cooking for so many. Once I've figured out the main course, my daughter Rachel helps plan all the sides and the dessert. She then rallies the other girls to choose what food they will bring. So most weeks all I do is the main dish. If it's a roast or a ham, I will probably also do the potatoes. But if it's something like lasagna, that's all I prepare, and the girls bring the rest.

MAKE-IT-YOURS TRADITIONS

I have come to view my Sabbath preparations as the most important thing I do all week (besides worship). I plan the menu as soon as I can, I shop, and then I try to prepare as much of the meal as possible on Thursday or Friday. Spreading out the labor means that I am not exhausted by the time everyone arrives.

Sabbath Dinner is a tradition you can establish. You can use your imagination to make it a party. Sometimes I sprinkle candies down the younger kids' table. Around Christmas they get a mandarin orange by their plate. My husband has written a liturgy for our family that includes asking each grandchild a question, singing, a prayer, and a blessing on the children and on me. They have it down by heart.

During Advent the liturgy includes me lighting an Advent candle, and on Christmas Day I light the candle in the middle of the Advent ring. Once you begin a regular Sabbath Dinner, you will be surprised at how it just seems to come together in a way that is uniquely yours. As you do this together by faith and with a lot of hard work, you will be blessed and your children's children will be blessed. And that's really why we do it.

CHAPTER 10

Living in Community

"**I** therefore, the prisoner of the Lord, beseech you to walk worthy of the calling with which you were called, with all lowliness and gentleness, with longsuffering, bearing with one another in love, endeavoring to keep the unity of the Spirit in the bond of peace" (Eph. 4:1–3).

Many things can threaten the unity of the Spirit in your family and in your church community. When you have disunity in your family, it can spread to the church. If you have disunity in the church, it can spread to the family. But in this passage above we are beseeched to endeavor to keep the unity of the Spirit in the bond of peace. This is strong language.

Paul is almost begging us to work hard to keep and protect this spiritual unity. And if you look at how we are to do this, you'll see that it requires some heavy lifting: we must be lowly, gentle, and longsuffering. So far this is not very glamorous. He does not say that we must be right or forceful or persuasive. Rather, we must be willing to put up with a lot, and do so in a loving manner. So to sum it up, living in community and enjoying unity requires that we put others first. This is a tall order, and Paul doesn't even call this "super-duper-level Christianity." He calls it walking worthy of the calling we have received as Christ's followers.

Matthew Henry's commentary says of this verse in Ephesians, "We do not walk worthy of the vocation wherewith we are called if we be not faithful friends to all Christians, and sworn enemies to all sin." I would like to add that we should be sworn enemies to our own sins first. And really, if we are at war with our own sins, we will find it far easier to deal with the sins of others.

FAMILY FIRST

The first unity we want to protect and keep is the unity we have with our married children and grandchildren. In the chapter on the mother-in-law I addressed some of the threats to this unity, the chief one being chasing your married children away with the stick of obligations, expectations, and comparisons. Rather, we must follow Naomi's example to set our children free to create their own homes, traditions, and culture, while we assume a supportive role.

EXTENDED FAMILY

In our church community many of our young married couples have both sets of parents living in the same town. Not only that, but their married siblings also have both sets of parents in town. So quite a few of my friends have two or more married children in town, and all those in-law children have their own parents in town as well. Can you imagine how this might create tension? That is why we must strive to preserve the unity.

One of the obvious points of conflict involves the holidays, and I have talked with wives who live under such a heavy burden from one or both sets of parents that it spoils the joy of celebrating Easter, Thanksgiving, and Christmas. When parents are insisting it is "their turn" to have them for Christmas, it simply turns Christmas into an obligation, and not a very fun one.

Rather, to preserve the unity, we must be open-handed. We must set our children free to celebrate however they want to. But what if this leaves you and your husband home alone for Christmas? Better that than a house full of children who were "guilted" into coming. You remember the proverb: "Better is a dinner of herbs where love is, than a fatted calf with hatred" (Prov. 15:17).

Not only that, but we must also be flexible and open-hearted about how we celebrate. I have one friend who has accommodated her married children by celebrating Christmas with them a day early, the morning of Christmas Eve. They look forward to being at her home as the kick-off to Christmas. The key is to be creative, imaginative, and generous. If your kids will be spending Christmas elsewhere, send them off without laying a guilt trip on them. Give them their gifts early or mail them to where they'll be staying as a surprise. The point is to protect the unity. Put their interests ahead of your own.

Remember, this requires lowliness of mind, and there is only one place where we can find such an attitude. You should care more that your children enjoy their own Christmas, their own way, than you care about your own celebration of Christmas. This means laying it all on the altar and letting it go.

I guarantee you that God does not bless coerced celebrations of the Advent of His Son. Why should He? But He blesses open-hearted generosity and a spirit of humility

SHARING THE GRANDKIDS

All of what I have written above holds true with the grandkids as well. You may not, you must not, keep track of how much time the other grandparents are getting. You must not compare gifts or compete for time or be jealous over them. It is entirely possible that it has never occurred to your grandkids to compare you to their other grandma. Don't teach them how to do this. Rather, be positive about the other grandparents. Appreciate the culture that is being handed down from the other side of the family. Don't be critical.

Friendship with your co-grandparents is a lovely thing. So if possible, promote it. But if it just doesn't happen, don't worry about it. Strive for love and peace and be satisfied with those things.

LOVING THE SAINTS

If we have practiced unity in our homes and unity in sharing our children and grandchildren, we will be prepared to let this extend to the saints in our churches and in our communities. As older women, we should be setting an example of lowliness and kindness to others, endeavoring to get along with our brothers and sisters in Christ. Consider Paul's exhortation to Euodias and Syntyche (Phil. 4:2–3), two women in Philippi who were not getting along.

Whatever their disagreement, it had gotten so bad that the apostle had to speak to it publicly, asking the church to help those women to "be of the same mind as the Lord."

In any Christian community, large or small, there will be many provocations and many occasions to sin against one another. Lowliness of mind is going to be the means that God uses to help us keep the peace.

LOWLINESS

Lowliness runs in stark opposition to pride, so this means we work hard to act and not react. If we are lowly, we are not easily offended. We will not count up wrongs, or store up in our heart the occasions when we felt slighted, overlooked, or outright wronged. We "put up with" the weakness and problems of others, not ceasing to love them because it has gotten hard. We find fresh grace to apply in every instance of provocation and don't let an angry word slosh out of an angry heart.

Even the godliest of Christians can be a provocation to one another. It turns out we all have rough edges. So we must bear with one another and resist the temptation to get even, returning evil for evil. If you are truly wronged, then you have been given a wonderful opportunity to apply your Christianity. Don't give up loving people because they are not always lovable. We are not always lovable ourselves. Forgive as you want to be forgiven.

You may differ with your in-law children or their parents on many things, but that does not mean you have to make it an issue. We simply have to remember what we have in common: unity in Christ. So you look for ways to keep it. After all, it is the bond of peace which binds us all together, not our views on politics or childbirth or homeschooling.

"There is one body and one Spirit, just as you were called in one hope of your calling; one Lord, one faith, one baptism; one God and Father of all, who is above all, and through all, and in you all" (Eph. 4:4–6).

The great alternative to disunity is to imitate Christ.This is going to require boots-on-the ground, practical Christian living.

Ephesians 4:32: "And be kind to one another, tenderhearted, forgiving one another, even as God in Christ forgave you."

HINDRANCES

The things that get in the way of harmony and unity in the Christian community are always sin. Here are a few examples.

Lying: When you say you'll do something, and you don't, this is a form of lying. When you change what you said to make you look or sound better, this is sin. We must love the truth and speak the truth.

"Therefore, putting away lying, 'Let each one of you speak truth with his neighbor,' for we are members of one another" (Eph. 4:25).

Anger: When you react or fly off the handle and speak in anger, this is inviting the enemy in. You may try to justify it because of the offense of the other person, but anger does not serve God's purpose. Extend forgiveness instead.

"'Be angry, and do not sin:' do not let the sun go down on your wrath, nor give place to the devil" (Eph. 4:26–27).

Stealing: We have first-hand experience of Christians stealing from us. But there are other ways to steal besides having something taken from your home. You steal by driving a hard bargain. You steal when you don't pay your bills. You steal when you borrow something and don't return it. This puts distance between you and your brother or sister. I have talked with Christians who do not like to do business with fellow Christians because they ask for a cheaper price or they don't pay their bills. I am afraid this is a fairly widespread problem. Shouldn't we be eager to pay our fellow Christians full price rather than rob them? Take care of any outstanding debts and restore the broken relationship.

"Let him who stole steal no longer, but rather let him labor, working with his hands what is good, that he may have something to give him who has a need" (Eph. 4:28).

Bad mouthing: When we run down others, we are pulling apart not building up. Don't do it and don't listen to it. Use your words to build up and not to tear down. Be careful of passing on information that might not be accurate or kind.

"Let no corrupt word proceed out of your mouth, but what is good for necessary edification that it may grace the hearers" (Eph. 4:29).

All-round badness: All sin is disruptive and destructive. If we want to preserve the unity in the Christian community, we will live like Christians. We will imitate Christ. We will quit inviting sin into our lives and replace it all with true Christian humility.

"Let all bitterness, wrath, anger, clamor, and evil speaking be put away from you, with all malice" (Eph. 4:31).

CHAPTER 11

Physical and Spiritual Health

"**B**eloved, I pray that you may prosper in all things and be in health, just as your soul prospers" (3 John 2).

The Apostle John prays for prosperity "in all things" for Gaius, the recipient of this epistle, particularly that he will be in health. Though we all appreciate good health, we know that a soul that is prospering is far to be preferred. Do what we might, our physical health will some day give way, and there will be not one thing we can do about it. But our spiritual health is something we can steward and nourish until our dying day.

John's prayer for prosperity is something we should pray for one another and for ourselves. We want to be healthy in body and thriving spiritually. We want God to prosper the work of our hands. But if we look closely at this prayer, we see John prays that Gaius' life will be just as prosperous as his soul. His soul sets the standard of health and takes the precedence here.

What if God instantly gave you physical health to match your soul's health? Would your physical health improve? Or would you suddenly get sick? This might give us pause to think. Clearly, our priority is to be spiritually healthy and prospering.

"For bodily exercise profits a little, but godliness is profitable for all things, having promise of the life that now is and of that which is to come" (1 Tim. 4:8).

We often find great courage and faith displayed at the deathbeds of the saints. This means that while their body was failing, their souls were prospering. Spiritual health enables the sick to deal patiently and victoriously with poor physical health.

"A merry heart does good, like medicine, but a broken spirit dries the bones" (Prov. 17:22).

Spiritual health can affect our physical health, and vice versa. This is a mystery. Though we can invest much money and time on things to improve our physical health, we would be foolish to pursue these things to the exclusion of our soul's health. Our goal should be to pursue spiritual health first, and not allow the world's preoccupation with physical health to distract us.

SPIRITUAL HEALTH

"Only take heed to yourself, and diligently keep yourself, lest you forget the things your eyes have seen, and lest they depart from your heart all the days of your life. And teach them to your children and your grandchildren" (Deut. 4:9).

We each know better than anyone how we are really doing spiritually. We can cover it, camouflage it, or pretend we are doing better than we really are, but it will eventually come out if we are getting spiritually flabby or sickly. Take heed to yourself. Keep your soul with diligence and oversight. How do we do this? What is it to have spiritual vitality? What can we do to keep our souls diligently?

1. We can be Bible readers, and not merely readers but doers.

2. We can worship God on the Lord's Day, sit under faithful preaching, take the Lord's Supper, and sing psalms and hymns.

3. We can keep short accounts with God, being quick to repent.

4. We can not tolerate sin in our own hearts, and confess to those we sin against.
5. We can be faithful in daily prayer.
6. We can love the fellowship of the saints.
7. We can be generous with all God has given us.
8. We can be faithful to remember and obey all God's commands.
9. We can rejoice in trials.
10. We can be content with what God is doing in our lives, giving thanks for all things.

Now the Christian life is not a list of ten things to do. And as I have said before, the Christian life is simple to understand but hard to do. I have simply listed these things as ways to take your spiritual temperature. Are you thriving? If so, the list above probably describes your spiritual life. If it doesn't, then your soul may not be prospering. In that case, take action.

What causes our spiritual health to deteriorate? Lots of things, but here is a short list of possible causes.

1. *Coasting.* You may think you've read your Bible enough already, and you've lost interest. Or church has become something you don't look forward to any more.
2. *Discontent.* This is the state of unhappiness that comes of dwelling on the things you wish were

different rather than thanking God for things as they are.

3. *Opinions.* If you care more about what others think of you than what Christ thinks of you, then your soul is in peril. People-pleasing is not what we are called to, and what pleases people is seldom what pleases God.

4. *Idolatry.* If your relationships are more important to you than your spiritual life, then they are on a pedestal where only God belongs.

5. *Forgetting.* We must remind ourselves of what God has told us to remember. When we drift, forgetfulness takes root.

6. *Worldliness.* If we are not paying attention, the world will press us into its mold. We must be diligent, thoughtful, careful. Matthew Henry, in his book The Quest for Meekness and Quietness of Spirit, says this: "And therefore Christians, whatever you have of the world in your hands, be it more or less, as you value the peace as well as the purity of your souls, keep it out of your hearts."*

7. *Tolerating little sins.* A little lie, a little gossip, a little anger, a little covetousness, and soon we have a big backlog of sin. Don't tolerate

---

* Matthew Henry, *The Quest for Meekness and Quietness of Spirit* (Morgan, PA: Soli Deo Gloria, 1996), 134.

these things. There really is no such thing as a little sin.

PHYSICAL HEALTH

Let's be honest: sometimes we spend a great deal more thought and care and anxiety over our physical health than we do about our spiritual health.

Our national idol of health care is toppling, and this is unsettling because we put way too much hope and trust in what medicine can do for us. The truth is, we tend to care more about someone when they are sick than when they are not doing well spiritually.

As a nation, we spend time, energy, and truckloads of money on all kinds of things that will supposedly keep us healthy. We worship health and fitness. And though physical exercise is fine in its place, it is not more important than spiritual exercise. We are very "in touch with" our bodies, tracking our weight and counting our steps, watching what we eat and taking our vitamins. But how in touch are we with our hearts and souls? Are we keeping our souls as diligently as we are keeping our bodies? Are we taking heed to our souls as much as we are taking heed to our bodies?

At the same time, Jesus does not dismiss our bodies as irrelevant. He cared very much for the sick, and much of His ministry involved healing those with various ailments. He is compassionate and kind. He does not tell us to ignore our bodily ailments, but rather we are to pray for healing and help. As we grow older, our ailments are going to increase. This is the way it is, and we can't change it. Everything is falling apart! But in the meantime, we can thank God for our health, enjoy our health, and use it for His kingdom work. Health is a tremendous asset and a wonderful gift from God. So I am not suggesting that we quit thinking about our physical health. Rather, I am suggesting we should give our souls more than equal time.

Remember to keep your soul. If you tend to your soul, when illness comes, you will be in much better shape to handle it.

CHAPTER 12

Stewarding Affliction

Though everyone must learn to steward affliction, we older women want to demonstrate to our children and grandchildren what this looks like. In other words, when we have a trial, we want them to see us using it to turn a spiritual profit. The end result is that we are richer for it, which means they have a richer inheritance for it.

"My brethren, count it all joy when you fall into various trials, knowing that the testing of your faith produces patience. But let patience have its perfect work, that you may be perfect and complete, lacking nothing" (Jas. 1:2–4).

So how do we turn a profit on trials and afflictions? In the passage above, James says our first response to trials should be joy. This is counter-intuitive. It seems the first response should be shock, dismay, sorrow, and misery. That is what the flesh tells us. But God wants us to look past the trial in front of us and know that He has sent it for a good purpose. In that knowledge, we can rejoice.

TESTING

No matter what kind of trial it is, whether poor health or financial hardship, all our trials are designed particularly for us by a good and loving Father. He knows what our souls need, and apparently our souls need a test from time to time.

A test is an opportunity to demonstrate what you have learned. If you are taking a biology class, you are tested on the material. We all know how to take tests, and we know how to prepare: pay attention in class, do your homework, and review.

When God gives us a test, it is always an open-book test. We have His Word available to us all the time. We are to be learning the material, paying attention, and reviewing. A pop test may surprise us, but we should be ready. We have the Book.

If we consider trials as a test, it may help us interpret them more positively. God wants to show us how our faith is doing. When we pass the test, we grow in patience and perseverance. We mature. Our faith grows. And we get another test over the new material. If we fail the test, we know we need to do more preparation, and we know God will give us another opportunity to do better next time.

JOY IN TRIALS

"I am exceedingly joyful in all our tribulation" (2 Cor. 7:4).

How does joy tie in with test-taking and tribulation? If we know the test is given for us and not to us, we can rejoice. We rejoice in the test because we know our faith needs to be tested. We rejoice in the Test-Giver who does all things well. We rejoice that our faith is not growing stagnant but is being tested, trained, strengthened, and fortified by the trials in our lives. This is how we turn a profit: we rejoice.

Look at Paul's prayer for the Colossians: "That you may walk worthy of the Lord, fully pleasing Him, being fruitful in every good work and increasing in the knowledge of God; strengthened with all might, according to His glorious power, for all patience and longsuffering with joy; giving thanks to the Father who has qualified us to be partakers of the inheritance of the saints in the light" (1:10–12).

The thing I want you to note is the connection patience and longsuffering have to joy. They go together. And notice also that the strength Paul is praying for is what equips them for patience and longsuffering. We need strength to be joyful. We need strength for trials. But what is this strength?

A POWERFUL TOOL

"Do not sorrow, for the joy of the Lord is your strength" (Neh. 8:10).

I hope you see that the strength Paul prays for the Colossians is the joy of the Lord. So in the midst of trials we need strength, right? And where do we find it? In the joy of the Lord. This is a wonderful truth and very practical. This enables us to find contentment in the midst of trials because we have learned that the joy of the Lord is our strength in adversity. He has not left us without hope in our afflictions, but He has given us a powerful tool: joy.

It turns out, affliction is one of the chief opportunities given to us for growth in grace and maturity in fruit-bearing. And joy is beautifying. We were created for joy. It transforms our attitude, our demeanor, our home, and our church. When we are able to find joy and contentment in our trials, we are beautifying the trials themselves and bringing glory to God.

Who is affected? We are. And our children and our grandchildren are blessed downstream.

CONTENTMENT

This is how we find contentment, not only in our difficult afflictions, but in the day-to-day petty annoyances that can trouble us. Contentment comes when we are satisfied with God's will in our lives. Discontent comes when we are not thankful for the things we do have, and when we want things that we do not have.

Paul says in Philippians, "Not that I speak in regard to need, for I have learned in whatever state I am, to be content" (Phil. 4:11). When he has things he doesn't want, he is content. When he doesn't have things he wants, he is content. This is definitely a learned skill. It does not come easily. It is so much easier to grumble and complain, compare and envy. But all those reactions are fleshly, worldly, and sinful, and they rob us of our joy.

The way to contentment is to do what pleases God by means of our obedience, and to be pleased with what He does by means of His providence. If you think about this, you'll see that it covers everything. And if we determine to please God and be pleased by God, this will keep us safe from many temptations.

JOY = STRENGTH

But though this sounds simple, it requires true spiritual strength. We find it hard to obey God and easy to indulge in self-pity. This is why we need a Savior. Rather than thinking about our wants or our hardships, we must set our minds on our mercies. Rather than comparing our condition to those who are better off, we must stir up gratitude. Things could be far worse.

If we really are Christ's disciples, then we must take up our cross and follow Him (Luke 9:23). This involves denying ourselves. However hard the trial might be, contentment will make it far more comfortable to endure. The contented heart pleases God and gives us victory over the circumstances and over ourselves. Remember, the joy of the Lord is our strength. He gives us joy in Himself and He gives us the strength to rejoice. A joyful heart is a contented heart.

CHAPTER 13

The Big Picture

Our culture is in love with immaturity. Most women don't really want to look their age after they turn twenty-five. But let's not think of ourselves as old, let's think of ourselves as mature and wise. That gives us something to live up to, something we should welcome and not shrink away from.

Getting older should not fill us with fear. We should be glad. It was my son who pointed out how dreadful it would be if we were running a race that had no end. A race with no finish line. That would be futility. Rather, we can rejoice that we have made it around another lap, getting closer to the end, but with still a distance to go.

God has given us promises about old age that we should commit to memory. He made us, carries us, delivers us, promises us fruitfulness, satisfies us, and adds peace to it all. What a kind Father we have, who does not desert us in our old age, but crowds us with blessings.

"Even to your old age, I am He, and even to gray hairs I will carry you! I have made, and I will bear; even I will carry, and will deliver you" (Is. 46:4).

"They shall still bear fruit in old age; They shall be fresh and flourishing" (Ps. 92:14).

"With long life I will satisfy him, and show him My salvation" (Ps. 91:16).

"My son, do not forget my law, but let your heart keep my commands; for length of days and long life and peace they will add to you" (Prov. 3:1–2).

With a blessed and long life, we know there will always be hardship as well. And that seems to be what causes most of our concerns. We worry about our health and possible ailments and diseases. We wonder what it will be like to be old and wrinkled, and it doesn't sound easy at all. Paul knows about this tendency we have, and he teaches us what is actually going on as our bodies fall apart.

"Therefore we do not lose heart. Even though our outward man is perishing, yet the inward man is being renewed day by day. For our light affliction, which is but for a moment, is working for us a far more exceeding and eternal weight of glory" (2 Cor. 4:16–17).

We don't need to pretend like this isn't really happening when it is. We are perishing. This is the true state of affairs. The KJV says we are "wasting away." But the good news is that the internal man is taken up in a process going the other direction. As our bodies weaken, our spirits gain strength.

This passage goes on to point out that the things we see (like our bodies) are temporary, but the eternal things are not visible to our eyes. And so we are to fix our eyes on what we can't see, on the invisible, not on the visible. We must see the invisible with the eyes of faith.

We see our visible afflictions with our eyes. We see our bodies wasting away and getting old. Varicose veins. Stronger lenses for our glasses. Weak hearts. Weak knees. But with our eyes of faith we see these afflictions are working for us. They are working something amazing: "a far more exceeding and eternal weight of glory" (vs. 17).

So how can we lose heart over aging when we know this is just for a moment. It is so short. And just when we thought our perishing bodies were working against us, Paul tells us they are actually working for us. They are working something we cannot even begin to know or understand, and yet we see it by faith.

And don't worry, Paul says. While our body is perishing, our spirits are being renewed each and every day. This is supernatural work that is going on in our inward man.

"Not by works of righteousness which we have done, but according to His mercy He saved us, through the washing of regeneration and renewing of the Holy Spirit" (Titus 3:5).

RENEWAL IS HOLY SPIRIT WORK, AND IT IS ONGOING WORK.

"But those who wait on the Lord shall renew their strength; they shall mount up with wings like eagles, they shall run and not be weary, they shall walk and not faint" (Isaiah 40:31).

"And do not be conformed to this world, but be transformed by the renewing of your mind, that you may prove what is that good and acceptable and perfect will of God" (Rom. 12:2).

Even though we must prepare for more changes to come, we don't need to fear. God is renewing and transforming us one day at a time. We wait on Him and He renews us and gives us new strength. Our minds are being renewed as we resist the world and submit to God.

So the conclusion is that we must continue to do our duties and stay at our posts. We don't need to start over or change course. Gradually, as God renews our hearts and minds, we gain spiritual strength even as we grow physically weaker. This is His way.

So as I conclude this little book for older women, I'd like to close with a little summary of practical advice for the days ahead.

Continue to be flexible as life changes. Remember that your husband is changing too. Pay attention to him. Don't let your relationship grow stagnant or static. Read a book. Improve your marriage. Take pleasure in delighting your husband.

The dynamic in your children's families will change as their children grow up and marry. Just when you got the whole Christmas thing worked out, something changed! Cultivate flexibility. Stay limber. Take things in stride.

NEVER QUIT CULTIVATING A GENTLE AND QUIET SPIRIT.

Don't be afraid of the future. Be unafraid of the changes ahead, unafraid of growing old. The holy women in Sarah's day were not afraid with any terror, nor should we be. We are in good company. We are to follow their good example. Be women of courage, women of faith.

Grow old gracefully. You can't become a whiny old lady if you are not whiny now. You can't become a grumpy old lady unless you are grumpy now. You can't become stuck in your ways and sure you are always right unless that is who you are now.

Keep your eye on the big picture. Focus on the invisible. Give yourself away until there is nothing left, and you will leave behind a legacy of a rich, exuberant, faithful family culture for your great-great-grandchildren after you.